# Meet the Dream Team

Barbie "Brooklyn" Roberts is visiting her BFF Barbie "Malibu" Roberts at the Dreamhouse. The two friends help each other work toward their dreams, getting into all kinds of fun along the way! Malibu, Brooklyn, their family, and their friends each bring new skills and attitudes to the Dreamhouse.

**Barbie "Brooklyn" Roberts:**
Fearless and smart, Barbie is a skilled singer, dancer, and musician who dreams big! She believes that practice and preparation are the keys to achieving her dreams. Sharing talents is one of her favorite ways to get to know new friends.

**Barbie "Malibu" Roberts:**
Barbie is strong, confident, and kind. She jumps at the chance to try something new, often finding herself in amazing situations! She learns from her mistakes and wants everyone to have their moment in the spotlight.

**Skipper:**
Tech-savvy Skipper puts on a cool face, but she secretly wants to gush about music, gadgets, and her dog.

**Stacie:**
Sporty and adventurous, Stacie likes to try new things and isn't afraid to fail! She's extremely competitive but would do anything for her sisters.

**Chelsea:**
Count on six-year-old Chelsea to set a story straight and make her sisters laugh. She is a tireless seeker of knowledge who asks a bazillion questions about everything.

**Ken:**
Supportive but goofy, Ken is Malibu's neighbor and oldest friend. He surfs, sails, and dives, and wants to become a marine biologist one day.

**Teresa:**
Thoughtful Teresa proudly shares her smarts. Her friends rely on her for level-headed advice, but she is happiest chatting about science, technology, and cosplay.

**Renee:**
Renee has a need for speed! She enjoys running track, skateboarding, and skiing. She dreams of owning her own luge sled one day.

**Nikki:**
Nikki is an artist and designer. She designs clothes and outfits to express who she is. Her motto is, "Why be them when you can be you?"

**Daisy:**
The only thing Daisy loves more than music and dancing is making new friends. She's a talented DJ with a big heart.

# Sweet Surprises

Welcome to the heart of the Dreamhouse. Malibu and Brooklyn are trying out each other's recipes. Which sweet treats would you like to try?

Place a cupcake sticker next to each item you find.

# Bestie Bonus

What did Brooklyn teach Malibu to make?

# Fave Frenzy

Brooklyn and Malibu love discovering how they are similar and different. To share that with the world, they are filming a vlog of their favorite things. Can you find them in Malibu's room?

Place a gold star sticker next to each item you find.

# Bestie Bonus

Unscramble these letters to reveal each girl's favorite thing to share.

R D F P I S E H N I

# Paw-some Playtime

At an outdoor get-together with friends, the Roberts sisters are playing with their puppies. Taffy, DJ, Rookie, and Honey want to play fetch! Will someone throw the ball for them?

Place a ball sticker next to each item you find.

# Bestie Bonus

Who Am I? I am a shy dog,
I belong to Malibu, and
I am named after candy.

9

# The Quest for Knowledge

Why do bath toys float? How do plants grow? Chelsea wants to know everything, and the only way to learn is by asking questions and doing experiments. Brooklyn and Malibu have invited Teresa and Renee over to help Chelsea with her experiments.

Place a heart sticker next to each item you find.

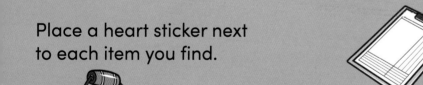

# Bestie Bonus

Can you fill in the blanks to name the living organism that grows with water and sunlight?

| | L | | N | |
|---|---|---|---|---|

Make sure to have parent supervision when doing your own experiments at home!

# Music Practice

Daisy is going to perform at a music fair at Chelsea's school, and she's asked her friends to join her band. They are practicing outside of the Dreamhouse before they visit the school. Preparation is the key to success!

# Bestie Bonus

What's this object where you can write the lyrics to your songs?

Place a backpack sticker next to each item you find.

# Pizza Party

Stacie is hosting a pizza party for her soccer team. Malibu and Skipper helped her pick pizza toppings and Brooklyn is in charge of the playlist. Search the living room for all the items Stacie needs to create the most delicious party.

Place a pizza slice sticker next to each item you find.

# Bestie Bonus

Can you fill in the blanks to name this popular pizza topping?

P _ _ P E _ O _ _

# Doctor Skipper

Skipper is dreaming about the future. With her love of science and animals, she wants to try being a veterinarian! Skipper asks DJ's vet if she can have a tour of the exam room, and she brings Malibu and Brooklyn along with her. Skipper learns what happens when her puppy gets a checkup!

# Bestie Bonus

Unscramble these letters to reveal what a vet uses to measure an animal's weight.

C L S E A

Place a paw print sticker next to each item you find.

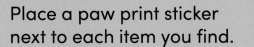

17

# Just Chillin'

After a long morning of kicking around the soccer ball, Renee and Stacie have just joined their friends by the pool. Can you find items that will make their sunny day relaxing?

Place a smoothie sticker next to each item you find.

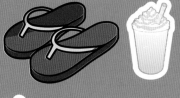
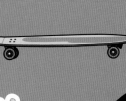

# Bestie Bonus

Can you identify this sun-shading accessory?

# Practice, Practice, Practice

Brooklyn, Malibu, and Nikki are taking turns practicing for their upcoming dance audition. As Brooklyn practices her pirouettes, Malibu and Nikki give her encouraging advice to make sure that her routine is perfect!

Place a ballet shoes sticker next to each item you find.

# Bestie Bonus

What do you call the applause at the end of a show?

# Reach for the Stars

Malibu's latest passion is astronomy. She and Brooklyn are learning all about space on her computer. What do you know about our cosmos?

Place a star sticker next to each item you find.

# Bestie Bonus

Unscramble these letters to reveal how many planets are in our solar system.

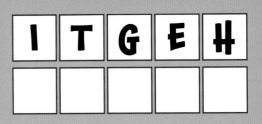

| I | T | G | E | H |
|---|---|---|---|---|
|   |   |   |   |   |

# Dance Party

Daisy is practicing her DJ skills by creating an impromptu dance party for her music-loving friends. Do you like to express yourself through song and dance?

Place a disco ball sticker next to each item you find.

# Bestie Bonus

When they work together, Malibu and Brooklyn make the best team. Unscramble these two words that define their friendship.

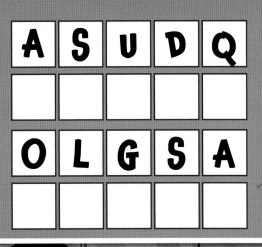

| A | S | U | D | Q |
|---|---|---|---|---|
|   |   |   |   |   |
| O | L | G | S | A |
|   |   |   |   |   |

# Inhale, Exhale

Malibu, Brooklyn, and their friends are doing yoga in the backyard to improve their strength, balance, and flexibility. What exercise do you enjoy?

Place a water bottle sticker next to each item you find.

# Bestie Bonus

Who am I? I am Malibu's oldest friend and a beach-loving surfer.

27

# Sleep Tight, Besties

Malibu and Brooklyn's friends are joining them for a sleepover at the Dreamhouse! Sleepovers are the best time to share feelings and dreams. Who would you like to have a sleepover with?

Place a cushion sticker next to each item you find.

# Bestie Bonus

Unscramble these letters to find an object that helps lead to a peaceful sleep.

L W P L O I

## Sweet Surprises 4-5

Bestie Bonus: Carrot cake

## Fave Frenzy 6-7

Bestie Bonus: Friendship

## Paw-some Playtime 8-9

Bestie Bonus: Taffy

## The Quest for Knowledge 10-11

Bestie Bonus: Plant

## Music Class 12-13

Bestie Bonus: Notebook

## Pizza Party 14-15

Bestie Bonus: Pepperoni

## Doctor Skipper 16-17

Bestie Bonus: Scale

## Just Chillin' 18-19

Bestie Bonus: Sunglasses

## Practice Makes Perfect 20-21

Bestie Bonus: Standing ovation

## Reach for the Stars 22-23

Bestie Bonus: Eight

31

Bestie Bonus: Squad goals

Bestie Bonus: Ken

## Sleep Tight, Besties     28–29

Bestie Bonus: Pillow